REVEAL

REVEAL:
All Shapes & Sizes

BRUCE COVEY

Bitter Cherry Books
Atlanta, GA
2011

Grateful acknowledgement is made to the editors and publishers of the following journals and anthologies in which parts of this book first appeared: *can we have our ball back?, Explosive Magazine, CrossConnect, GlitterPony, Gutcult, Puppyflowers, Word For/Word, Ampersand, Softblow, Ligature, Kulture Vulture, Shampoo, No Tell Motel, Anemone Sidecar, Traverse, Cranky, The Hat, Unpleasant Event Schedule, the tiny, dusie, 42opus, Alice Blue, horse less review, ActionYes, St. Elizabeth Street, Otoliths, CAB/NET, Coconut, Sawbuck,* and *Wherever We Put Our Hats.*

REVEAL

REVEAL 1: **Planet**

Mercury: Take a look at where we're headed

Venus: There's a lot you can see with very modest equipment

Earth: You'll come across a page which explains how to proceed

Mars: Looking for information about spirit and opportunity

Jupiter: Access limited to clients and guest users

Saturn: Take a closer look at the vehicles above

Uranus: The important thing is not to stop questioning

Neptune: In the long run men hit at only what they aim

Pluto: Mapping out a strange, curly path of light and dark

Sedna: The comets we see are strong evidence

REVEAL 2: **Zodiac**

Rat: You will have a cancellation due to schedule restraints

Ox: A gene causing childhood will be identified

Tiger: Plans are under way to restore your reign

Rabbit: Even breeding a single time can have consequences

Dragon: Save time & money; implement unique speech technologies

Snake: Collect blue starts; collect red question marks. Never miss another call

Horse: Avoid disputes with equine leases. Add an event

Goat: Adjust factors for milk records; fence

Monkey: Stay gold, cute, & on target. Shoot the evil kangaroo.

Rooster: Add value to your supply chain participants

Dog: You will return the best results from leading engines

Pig: Collect and process semen.

REVEAL 3: **Element**

home did

welcome map for news arts safari code up

search offers help join for about search go

conquer solution schools base free us social the look-alikes site for zinc regions information athletic personal storm bloodbath delay analyze your revolution clearing where press music at real and additional windows rent the general theories decision zero you crossword statistics announces an experience panther phase in farmers your well time pages and policy programs rise enter the wave spot at millimeter immediately commercial works club a brief description manifesto of famous reactions

its wire office science clean language dynamic acute philosophical design alarmed downloads separated of shown package with that quantity trend frequently are internet of section feet is new

REVEAL 4: **Baseball**

Pitcher: Please travel over to have a closer look
Catcher: View sample pages from this book
First Base: What to look for during play?
Second base: Is something incorrect, broken, or frustrating?
Third base: Numerals in various bases may look different
Shortstop: We haven't closed our doors in over 20 years
Left field: Look under our games section for screen shots
Centerfield: I wouldn't mind seeing a switch at the # 2 spot
Right field: Give lost out-of-towners crummy directions

REVEAL 5: **Day**

Sunday: Bad news for clock watchers; school bans all skirts

Monday: This interview was created via a series of postcards

Tuesday: Keep telling yourself: Above all, it's just a phone

Wednesday: The Michelin man from hell, a priest of yeast, the goddess in an apron

Thursday: When tickets officially go on sale, the early bird will expire

Friday: We'll be working hard to resolve the issue in time for next week's email

Saturday: Share your thoughts with others; adjust to user behavior

REVEAL 6: Fate & Fury

Clotho: Spinning wheel covers; check out different colors
Lachesis: The village rat home
Atropos: For migrant news as it happens
Alecto: To slot a green modeling van seems odd
Megaera: Frame break out: There are 73 more days
Tisiphone: Cite, rate, or print

REVEAL 7: Color

Black: Marjorie Stewart Joiner patented the permanent wave machine
White: Treasury Secretary John Snow discussed the economy
Red: Partner solutions. Deploy the applications you already use
Yellow: Decide how much to pay; send a free postcard
Blue: Official bubblin' ring tone hot property in Italy
Orange: 2 for 1 tickets for coaches every timeline
Green: Seeing their products graded red prompts them to do the right thing
Purple: I'm at a loss. What do other people think?
Pink: The achievement of establishing individuality is extraordinary
Brown: Voters sharply divide, over-propose casinos
Grey: How much does it cost? How can I give something back?

REVEAL 8: **Card**

Ace: Tao overview; zen overview; commercial support

2: Some crude humor, a brief substance reference

3: A four-day adrenaline-pumping party

4: That nice waiter is playing tricks to get you to fork

5: You may see a warning dialog box

6: Whether you're traveling for work or fun

7: Keep your favorites; take advantage

8: You draw her boobs & she calls it art

9: 80 second challenge: Which wine with pizza?

10: People with limited capacity will be encouraged

Jack: To find out more about responsible consumption

Queen: Click on through for all the news and gossip

King: Materials may not be reproduced

Heart: Soon your curiosity may lead to respect

Diamond: Already own a card?

Spade: You've been increasingly unreachable

Club: Follow in the footsteps of Lewis and Clark

REVEAL 9: Currency

Now: Don't gamble with rights; come to Las Vegas

Penny: Their payload has been delivered
Nickel: Click mass number for decay process
Dime: Complete with lurid cover illustration
Quarter: Enter your horseback riding hours
Dollar: And get the latest details on special offers

Amp: Eliminates needs for manual polishing
Volt: Captures the untethered quantity outlet
Watt: Information for current students, waiters
Ohm: Stresses learning by rote and the natural sun

REVEAL 10: Powers of Ten

One: Bluebird, blue*, bird, bl????rd, bl:snow

Ten: Please select your city from above

Hundred: Shatterproof is not a challenge

Thousand: They create shower curtains

Million: Includes people who are still living

Billion: Thank you for being visitor 1104682

Trillion: Wide area networks for the last mile

Quadrillion: Something different in the long & short

Quintillion: Scales laid out flat like a carpet

Sexillion: Get that dot while it's hot

…Nonillion: No tomatoes. Electric wheelchair

…Vigintillion: See also arrow, a table, gesundheit

…Googol: A mish-mash of eclectic destinations

…Googolplex: My page has disappeared into the byte void

REVEAL 11: Sin

Pride: Viva Judo! Deep impact! Deep official!
Envy: Success didn't go to his head
Wrath: Get a free dragon from the chaos realm
Sloth: Bid on seized coins, sausage slices, and jerky
Avarice: A snapshot's taken from the repository
Gluttony: Sabotage ruled out in dead dove incident
Lust: Would it do with the vocals possessed?

REVEAL 12: Range

Soprano: Circles the wagons, turns up the heat
Alto: Dust hazard reduced to zero; here you get a list
Tenor: Beyond the gadgets, a tsunami parade
Baritone: I have consulted two-dozen books to understand
Bass: What Rhonda brings to the maestro's table!

REVEAL 13: **Season**

Spring: Challenge the biologists of the new millennium
Summer: To the magical desert of Death Valley
Fall: It's a little blurry in places but most of it's okay
Winter: Why not spend the night?

REVEAL 14: Shape

Point: Massage chairs; mortgages; Los Angeles colocation

Segment: I'm mailing my vote from anywhere to anyone

Line: Are you a native speaker of Estonian or Lithuanian?

Circle: A very special being straight from the stars?

Ellipse: A ray of focus will pass through the other

Triangle: What's the best film you've seen lately?

    Which theater has the worst seats?

Square: Sign up today to be a pocket-sized reader

Rectangle: The spiral is not actually tangent at these points

Rhombus: If you would like to try and discover them

Pentagon: The nerve command is virtually a city within itself

Hexagon: Wee puns of mass distraction will run about

Dodecahedron: Appear as part of the staircase being ascended

REVEAL 15: **Muse**

Calliope: See the music, read the lyrics

Urania: Who never asked questions as to how, what, why?

Clio: Decode gold content in chocolate projects

Terpsichore: For stimulation, solve crossword puzzles

Melpomene: Girls are often relegated to traditional domestic spheres

Thalia: Press to watch using peace and harmony

Euterpe: Zooming, this version can export trees to pictures

Erato: This is a temporary mini-site to keep you

Polyhymnia: View programs and notes

REVEAL 16: Quark

Up: Report railroad emergencies
Down: You have risen again and given your all
Strange: Your body is creating and killing
Charmed: After trying on a pair of go-go boots
Bottom: Music spans the pool tables
Top: When only the hottest will do, rouse

REVEAL 17: **Beauty**

Finding your felons home notice
Dating is what's allowed lowest
Read it mailing love required
A standing add gallery fan
Free my perfect library fashion
A spectrum message requests playing
Ten series naughty note images
Buy angels foot the kisses
Film for independent gray hairspray
News icon, browse with questions

REVEAL 18: **Truth**

Spies are not contributors to democratization
Since 12:23 am, 21 people have died a tobacco-related death
Andy Kaufman is alive!
Use eggs to treat burn fictions
Climate changes threaten the human race
Hystericanes follow a regular cycle
Unmonitored teens are more likely to engage in risky behaviors
Static electricity can spark fuel fires
In video there can be no truth or falsity

REVEAL 19: **Chess**

Pawn: Write strategy notes to yourself

Knight: The founder and operator of real cities

Bishop: Selects departmental notices at left

Rook: If you are put off by maddeningly complex conventions

Queen: Time is the future in a place once called earth

King: Go to games together and keep a diary

REVEAL 20: Scale

Do: Renovate your bathroom into the ultimate retreat!
Re: Kingdom hearts or greater are absolutely positive!
Mi: New farm market ag tourism directory available!
Fa: Rover's tough toffee tie! Karen's red hot!
So: Flatten your abs? The wild goose chase ends here!
La: It's not just a train trip, it's a state of mind!
Ti: 1,000,000 digital radio chips shipped!
Do: Everything you need to build a stage!

REVEAL 21: **Chance**

Heads: Rhino offers them on platters of drugs called electricity
Tails: But how does wrapping a piece of paper over a rock destroy it?

REVEAL 22: **Distance**

Inch: Relocation is complete. Work has begun
Foot: The right place to find and be found
Yard: Disrupting traffic and parking arrangements
Mile: Newsreel coverage made a star out of love

Millimeter: What's in the box?
Centimeter: Metacognition elicits meaningful enhancements
Meter: The problem of worms raiding the background is a serious one

REVEAL 23: **Ennead**

Atum: An infinite stream must be placed on a board

Shu: The height from which Washington surveyed his troops

Tefnut: A woman lies horizontally between

Geb: The phenotype to fitness mapping is emergent

Nut: Teachers to be freed; signs up to music

Osiris: For a bronze, check out the dew tour

Isis: The menu slides trees, 123 zoos & aquariums

Set: & the game isn't over till the kings go wild!

Nephthys: We must understand that portion of the sky

REVEAL 24: **Tone**

Pitch: The shy guys explode
Duration: A red lever tips vanilla
Intensity: Dishes are broken. Loose bricks fall from buildings
Timbre: Translation is the source of the peephole

REVEAL 24: **Triangle**

Equilateral: Get a shot at the estimated pool
Isosceles: Its tunnel number is a knot
Scalene: Traffic jam's released; concentrics updated
Right: Geek superhero will warn you about changes
Acute: High fever, headache, overall feeling of discomfort
Obtuse: The matilda team offers a high availability grid
Oblique: Over one hundred worthwhile dilemmas

REVEAL 26: Art

Every few years someone dreams of making money
In other words: dead ones
A winner should be announced in the coming weeks
If you are updating your classroom
Young girl reading oil on paperboard
New nerves are extended only to the living
In particular through the device of slight raptures
Manufactured on the islands for use as caskets
The friendly alien investigates the starry night
The surroundings have adapted itself to the relief

REVEAL 27: **Sex**

Young vacationers are bringing home unwanted souvenirs
Older students help girls delay their first
Together for nearly 10, they separated after 5
The recent rally on the mall shows the deep support
She is quite far from a normal, ordinary young woman
Take a look back at your favorite defining moments
Designed to be viewed from above in true color
Buy books, literature, and tapes from conventions and medallions
As long as you turn your wife over to the cable guy
What offensive material is out there?

REVEAL 28: Movie

G: Don't throw anything away

PG: Vote Mr. Clean into Madison Avenue

PG-13: Do not use "the," "a," or "an"

R: Examine fertile cran-mirror education

NC-17: As the threesome becomes threatened

X: A perspective on the public and private sector

XXX: Includes neurons; other; tissues and organs

REVEAL 29: **Substance**

Animal: They are socializers and survivors. See one up close

Vegetable: You support banning arsenic and chromium from timber?

Mineral: Dazzling spheres are the big stuff

REVEAL 30: **Divine**

Inferno: Causing you to upstart suddenly, like a person
Purgatory: Where the dew washes off the stain and girds
Paradise: The outages will occur at the following times:

REVEAL 31: **Volume**

tsp: Calculators, returns & share prices, uniformed services

T: Give yourself amazing new powers! You'll do things like never before

oz: Express your feelings about six seasons

gi: Like about steps to take to prepare protect reserve

cup: Devoted exclusively to the study of lichens worldwide

pt: Spreading heifer, candidate to the city hall of Christmas

qt: Is pleased to release the first snapshot

gal: To advance the craft of string instrument making and repair

REVEAL 32: **Weight**

dr: Camel and banana coin problems doubling pennies grazing animals
oz: Gone but never forgotten. The unfortunate transition flash animated
lb: Amateur chefs turn up warnings and praise for turkey
cwt: Not itemized on the price tags of the goods we buy
ton: To commit to the timely publication of high-quality papers

REVEAL 33: Equation

A=πr^2: Choose the best answer to each of the following problems

e=mc^2: A somewhat unfamiliar conception for the average mind

ei$^\pi$-1=0: if (exceptionVector == 3 && (!(regs.eflags & 0x200)

C=2πr: Yes, that IS enough space to slide one finger in flatly

a^2+b^2=c^2: -d is impossible as you cannot have a negative dimension

x+y=1: That was too easy, wasn't it? Add me to your buddy list

REVEAL 34: Prime

1: Bug bounty matched dollar for dollar

2: The fairy godmother will keep you hooligans

3: Hot spot access: easy, seamless, & secure

5: Meet instantly with anyone, anywhere, anytime

7: 2 different platforms for the price of 1 strawberry

11: The true blue chain of kindness has your freebies

13: Dress like a star! What's your sign? Reach your goal

17: Duration, notice, deposit, infringement, remedies

19: Impart information regardless of frontiers

23: The official star bookmark of clowntrooper chaos

Africa: Look at my photo, what do u see?
Asia: Pool, mahjong, blackjack, literati blocks
Australia: Experience a different analog light
Europe: The involvement of men in reproductive health
S America: In a telephone sounds more approachable
N America: Investors may pack up and leave
Antarctica: Take it all in I do not believe

REVEAL 36: Blood

A: Wabbit parody about what happened in space

B: Prevents farmers' access to their lands

O: Light on theory, heavy on practical application

AB: How extreme is your machine? Enter

REVEAL 37: **Direction**

N: A library of blue ribbon content areas

NE: Bullying areas of expertise across the nation

E: Where's my car, hypes, hope, and hip-hop?

SE: DNA RNA protein conflict map

S: Unbiased analysis at your fingertips

SW: Destination: If you want to have great time

W: Host your own party at a local restaurant

NW: A monster promotion to Europe on sale

REVEAL 38: **Handedness**

Left: Coin the seating arrangement you see
Right: Around the root climb slightly

REVEAL 39: **Horseman**

War: May not find tons of mustard & nerve agents
Slaughter: The average live weight was 36 pounds
Famine: Theme Black 47, where tragedy is encapsulated
Death: Triangle, square, X, O

REVEAL 40: **Body**

Puddle: Spin you around, stop audio registration
Pond: Use our handy virtual, if you can't conveniently
Lake: A beehive, pioneers, seagulls, and the motto
Stream: What draws them in or drives them away
River: Really the summation of a whole valley
Sea: And sky invites you to explore inner space
Ocean: Here if you cannot see the above

REVEAL 41: **Work**

But garlic, licorice, & cucumber
That can be rolled up for storage?
Why must you shake down mercury?
It tears itself into countless little cubes
Helps you find & land & bushings into Bo Peep
To modernize & boost jobs & pensions.

Sending lava flows across the city
(Red, lower image) from the perspective
Of looking "heel" to find solid boards
After her supervisor handed out copies
The off-shoring wave is a depleting monster
Orange paid from your home can't find it?
What is an economical way to overcome
Geographical limitations? How over are you?

REVEAL 42: **Vowel**

A: A language is a dialect with an army

E: Answer, bitch! Talk tab fab, totally tube

I: An imaginary root is difficult to grasp

O: About as satisfying as a frozen microwave dinner

U: Boasting a basketball team that's small enough

Sometimes Y: A small splash in an even smaller pond

REVEAL 43: X

Professor: 60,000 students tell all

Cyclops: Didst leave the mountain nymphs, thy nurses

Angel: Thwart the supernatural creatures that prey

Storm: Ice is made from recycled bowling balls

Beast: Frustrated designers work in dark offices

Colossus: Where Xiaolin pocket bikes cluster

Wolverine: Multiply that mite some fifty times

Phoenix: Dirty projectors sell for $29.50

Nightcrawler: Get attention with a cool plot twist

Gambit: Kiss your chess obsession goodbye

Rogue: Amber is naked in a bathtub, a revolution

X-Men: In your opinion, what is the best thing about you?

REVEAL 44: **Temperature**

Fahrenheit: Eliminate fractions & increase granularity
Celcius: Heaven or hell it's your choice

REVEAL 45: **Time**

Instant: A witty gal who can engage me in ridiculous banter wink

Second: Some of the world's top professional table tennis players

Minute: Swap experience; another city breaks from 99 pounds

Hour: Pink flamingoes crack stateless code and deport

Day: They wander in an elliptical path and move more than 40

Week: Next 1 billion will be Chinese, Brazilian, Thai

Fortnight: Coconut smell whooshes me to the sand dunes

Month: Spider silk and spider poisons; the smell of jasmine flowers

Year: Apogee articles illustrate cliff's rocket science

Decade: Transmitter new horizons for FM applications

Century: Their punches can break your ribs

Millennium: Roll over map and click on a region

REVEAL 46: **Poker**

High: Wire plus line author equals Smith
Pair: The leftover circle-makers center
2 Pair: Matching products in the socks range
3 of a Kind: They've got a rotation of 5 grinders
Straight: Does ball lightning really exist?
Flush: In some ways nuts, but we hope clean
Full House: I think that's how a lot do so well
4 of a Kind: Snowboarding turning into fashion
Straight Flush: Later replaced by aquarius
Royal Flush: Magnets allow the ball to draw

REVEAL 47: Stooge

Moe: Dinner with the raffle winner announced
Larry: Copying is fine; cut & paste is not
Curly: You just might want to eat them up
Shemp: Find a woman in your area with dash
Joe: Instrumentation with strings and horns
Curly Joe: Leave flowers and a note for this person

REVEAL 48: Decade

20s: I'm your witchdoctor did it for you

30s: Cat number 4167, a pulp sourcebook

40s: The shadow, the whistler, and big swing

50s: Trivia, hangman, jigsaws, jumbles, checkers

60s: Psychedelic literary tradition & social change

70s: Do you remember Evel Knievel?

80s: All pouty and wearing something purple?

90s: Crash into me, everybody hurts. Criminal!

REVEAL 49: **Bean**

Green: Pacific pirate fishing rainbow warriors
White: Use every possible asset they have
Black: Like a cigarette, filter and all
Pole: Back home fat John feats freestyle
Lima: Evaluates agricultural subjects in TLC
Mung: Fractionally tarted-up fancy soup
String: Because objects are immutable they can be shared
Lentil: In the rain shadow of the cascade mountains
Refried: I am the little guru in your ear
Baked: Jumbled crossword, matching & gap-fill exercises
Coffee: Sometimes the black apron stirs you
Vanilla: Learn how I became the queen

REVEAL 50: (Moon) Phase

FM: Infected mushroom I'm the supervisor

NM: We hope you enjoy the new look and feel

FQ: Field standards include amplification documents

LQ: Join now and start earning points for free nights

REVEAL 51: **Death**

Over one million turkeys are raised each year
Getting away with distortion is out
A two-cigarette socket car adapter
Enables you to create a cloze activity in seconds!
Damage plan dime bag seven dust anthrax
Smaller centers and units interact
Sincerely might be celery
Sin on ornithological and scientific expeditions
I love mining cookies!
Go to imagine the universe in lingerie!

REVEAL 52: **Month**

January: He thinks his work will ultimately go out of fashion

February: Decisions relating to the siting of power

March: Every day 1 in 8 babies arrives too soon

April: With peasants pulling strands of spaghetti down from trees

May: Click here for a history of motions

June: The majority of the rose speculation occurs here

July: Special rates to visit American memory

August: With the legs to be around a long time

September: A museum to document the personal histories of red

October: Why not the alphabet and an automobile?

November: Show inclination to scrap sentencing

December: Put on your pajamas and dive

REVEAL 53: **Numeral**

I: Crossword and scrabble solvers, more translators, etc.

II: Fashionapple asks about Bangkok, "Hi friends"

III: This is to protect both of us and for training purposes

IV: A drip may be used to correct electrolyte imbalances

V: Such as Section 508 and the W3C's WCAG

VI: There is much more at the sane conference

VII: Pussycat doll auditions lost in Tokyo

VIII: Music pastime with good company

IX: Now 1,430,000 pages served per weekday

X: Eyes check out the parade behind the lucky mask

XX: Strategy weaving is for oppositional cyborgs

XXX: Rings and algebras, spectral theory

XL: For the hardest button to button is up

L: Within the framework of an image's support scheme

LX: Installing beautiful faces is a breeze

LXX: With truly orthodox notes for the 21st century

LXXX: Run to and fro like sparks among the stubble

XC: The option of displaying wind direction

C: One has great worm protection, the other promises death

D: I want to rent a tuxedo, not buy

M: He lures them into confidence with candy

REVEAL 54: **Nutrition**

Other: You can enter your weight in any unit you wish

Milk: With three NFL quarterbacks in the family

Meat: Pig escapes slaughterhouse, cow escapes slaughterhouse

Vegetable: They have some great ideas on freezing spinach

Fruit: Did you measure around the bust at apex?

Grain: Or, how corporations get their way

REVEAL 55: **Berries**

Straw: To find feeds, look for a white-on-orange icon

Blue: Ant joins ex-steps and the latch boy on the bench

Black: Our elevation must be the result

Rasp: Flesh & blood supermarket sweep identity

Boysen: Functional and trendy counters and screens

Cran: Every major seam is double-stitched for durability

Goose: 50-68 inches, sexes similar, large long-necked

Elder: To watch or not to watch?

Juniper: End-to-end layered plug-n-play deployment

Mul: Danger—keep off tracks electric current

Huckle: Data conversion of a too-large number

Halle: The zoo, botanical garden, race course, 1 in 5 cinemas

REVEAL 56: Offense

QB: Now all I need to do is get a chihuahua

HB: Flowing waterfalls, fish and dragonflies

FB: All the little roadblocks we have overcome

WR: How to prepare my home, business, and family?

WR: Affected by raging floods and mudslides

TE: The part that earthquakes and volcanic eruptions play

LT: Happy surfing don't forget

LG: Discover vacuum suction from the front & sides

C: We don't know how often you get over to Japan

RG: Now over 380 bullets and over 130 buttons

RT: I can only stand it for a short while

REVEAL 57: **Death (2)**

One can never look directly at the sun
Police and fireman stainless steel thank you cards
Reminder that life is slipping away second by second
Sharp disparities in eligibility by neighborhood
Has incorrectly listed someone as deceased
Forbidden knowledge, blue-blood paranormal anomalies
Then we'll see who's got the real problems
I've been a cabbie and a stock clerk and a soda-fountain jock-jerk
Morning light creeps across the eroded badlands
You may even eliminate the record you are seeking
The only compelling proof is out of body

REVEAL 58: **Utensil**

Knife: Grab one if you want because they won't last long
Fork: Time and time again we've challenged the multi-headed beast
Spoon: The infinite pet. The two sides of Monsieur Valentine
Chopsticks: It's now known that silver has no reaction to arsenic

REVEAL 59: Shade

Lavender: Lots of ways to pamper yourself

Puce: Envy to change, the ringing of your portable look

Violet: You can use it to draw contradictory diagrams

Fuchsia: Children die each week as a result of cruelty

Plum: The foot of the hill temple was established in 2003

Mauve: List for test patch suite submission

Magenta: Do something about it

Atomic: 0 pieces in your memo; Hi, my name is

Hydrogen: A stakeholder in Dennis Weaver, developing

Nitrogen: Lavera sun sprays, waterproof, mineral based

Cluster: Right out of the box, Beowulf puts a waffle

Rockeye: Dropping 15,828 of the 27,987 total

Car: To get a fair freefall deal & your life

Fuel Air: Well beyond the flattened area

Gator: & interests resulting in industry-leading kings

Dirty: Carried out w/the hand, space echo w/buckled hair

Daisy Cutter: To create an instant clearing in the jungle

Letter: To the Galatians & justification to ignite

Penetration: Moving targets with revamped packaging

    Sleeve notes cherry red for less than a fiver

Smart: What a parking lot! Always one step behind

GP: Merry Maid's housekeeping service?

Nuclear: Generally referred to as safeguards

Napalm: Against substrings conveyed in the crawler

Pulse: Through-hole and surface-mount power chokes

Time: Can stress help fight terrorism?

REVEAL 61: **Sense**

See: Six pence paths of the latest spirit
Hear: Out now: Who's not forgotten?
Touch: Teaching victory in metaphysical battles
Taste: Depolarizes until a threshold is reached
Smell: Connect the dots, the displaced fireworks

REVEAL 62: **Alphabet**

Alpha: Thinking of running a course?

Beta: Full stealth mode, anti-leak

Gamma: Power to rule the game

Delta: What's your reason?

Epsilon: Checking in with five-star

Zeta: Yellow tab is pleased to announce

Eta: Your rights as a worker

Theta: Once more recommend the nonpareil

Iota: Café seating is first come

Kappa: A mythical ball inside decorum

Lambda: Whilst we redevelop our drill court

Mu: It will surely blow your mind

Nu: Vagabonds mistakenly contribute to porno

Xi: For the purpose of improving

Omicron: The paper classroom on wheels

Pi: From one brim to the other

Rho: Contraceptive methods and eligibility criteria

Sigma: Please select a country

Tau: Extensive artificial intelligence

Upsilon: Predicts the ultimate place of

Phi: The golden section, ratio, or mean

Chi: All its functions have been taken over

Psi: By switching to the jabber network

Omega: Pressure, strain, force, flow

REVEAL 63: **Defense**

DE: Offerer on a search for new numbers

DT: After months of scrutiny we've modified the spokes

DT: To use with the orange learn button

DE: In front of the beach and two kilometers

OLB: Be the first to grow hair

MLB: Red birds open with an offensive outburst

OLB: When sleep forsakes his eyclids

CB: And guarantees the galaxy

SS: If you live abroad and cannot obtain paper

FS: Bring the American Chestnut back from near extinction

CB: For easy access to our huge selection

REVEAL 64: **Precipitation**

Rain: Are you willing to take the risk?
Sleet: The vertical line in the center of the diagram
Snow: Or perhaps you'd like to try your hand at
Hail: Punching the core—How bad can it get?
Freezing Rain: Most commonly found in a narrow band

REVEAL 65: **Balloon**

Weather: Every day brings something new
Mylar: Being extruded onto a chill roll
Animal: Prevents weapons from penetrating bodies
Latex: Consider the Cartesian price of eggs
Hot Air: Yes, there's room for another bomber
Rubber: A mysterious woman has telepathic powers
Water: Cultivates rice paddies, 5 pots a day
Speech: A burning angel for checkered content

REVEAL 66: **Nuts**

Wal: Sunbeam electric throw denim prairie
Pecan: As you've heard it said
Pea: We offer members advice on all matters
Coco: Shrewd, chic, and on the cutting edge
Macadamia: Some are smooth, but others are pebbled
Brazil: Distribution remains a pressing problem
Pine: Once upon a time, in 1889
Cashew: Fresh from the Yukon, furry and other
Almond: Science continues to learn more
Pistachio: Of shells that are not hard

REVEAL 67: Order

Doric: Voltage & current strain gauge test bench
Ionic: Select the red spider for their infrastructures
Corinthian: An increase of 55% over the prior year
Composite: Compared to traditional autoclave curing
Tuscan: Sexual content and language

REVEAL 68: Personality

Reformer: It's not just x-rays anymore
Helper: The transcontinental railroad elections theme unit
Motivator: Danced gleefully in the bright morning sunshine
Romantic: For puckering up those lips
Thinker: Search over 82,000 images
Skeptic: And buy the baloney detection kit!
Enthusiast: The latest and incredibly popular innovation is
Leader: Skimping starts on Day One
Peacemaker: Just point and beam

REVEAL 69: Comparison

Apple: Be firm and free of bruises and punctures
Orange: Plan to roam adaptively, Origami style

REVEAL 70: Apparel

Shirt: Come inside, you funny sheik

Pants: Rumor has it Schrodinger's Cat will celebrate

Skirt: For fewer wrinkles, for curlier hair

Dress: For their international support!

Jacket: A moment of strange lyricism

Underwear: Teensy Weensy and more

Sock: Implemented through the transport layers

Shoe: Female brands, male brands

Hat: The purple book has said it too

REVEAL 71: **Modern**

Williams: Have the lightning reflexes of a Formula One driver?

Stein: Happy birthday! Congratulations! A gift for you!

Hughes: Like speed, mathematics, and things mechanical?

Loy: Model train control of the future—here today!

Pound: And what is wrong with squid?

HD: Enough dreaming! It's time to ride!

Eliot: Does that suggest anything to you, sir?

Stevens: Add a third dimension to the structure!

REVEAL 72: **Curse**

Fuck: Board a loaded coal train for the long trip back
Shit: Increasingly, you can do it without wires too
Asshole: To read the odds of this flashing match
Damn: Via a method we call "trampolines"

Cock: You want funky brakes? Got it!
Pussy: Performing super feats of strength and daring
Piss: Arrive for dinner with your very own supply of ice
Hell: How fast is this a joke with results for real?

REVEAL 73: **Fabric**

Cotton: Salt tolerant and full of verve

Polyester: Lulu uses her macramé to strangle Sandra

Rayon: Large amounts of zinc in the spin bath

Linen: Dot the fields with violet umbrellas

Silk: Every vanilla has a sweetened story

Leather: Made of stars of mud and cans

Hemp: Stimulants, fans, blowers, pumps

Wool: I hate to have to say this but I do

REVEAL 74: Cube

1: Burning edge fire fox branch builds

8: From and inspired by the film

27: Quantum dot sources of photons on demand

64: Do you like fire red and leaf green?

125: The power car of the decade

216: 22½ feet of drywall

343: Comes to the steelworkers

512: Return of the beautiful

729: Outflow of worthless, elliptical

1000: How I cubed a cherry. Modern ruins

REVEAL 75: **Tense**

Past: That does not either vex or weary me
Present: Bath beads fishing lure lipstick
Future: Wish of the dead & the living

REVEAL 76: **Sandwich**

PBJ: They compose; they jockey; they direct

BLT: Other options let you rotate and scale

Reuben: Racecar is racecar backwards

Pastrami: After the fat is trimmed

Corned Beef: The country will spark many questions

Grilled Cheese: How gross is that?

Ham & Cheese: So that the strips alternate diagonally

Turkey: Surround the 4000-year-old ancient city

Chicken Salad: Humor them. Cut into diagonal quarters

Tuna Salad: Learn about a low dose hormone treatment

Egg Salad: A little special touch in the standard

French Dip: Within a mile of Dodger Stadium

Monte Cristo: And in a hostile medieval setting!

Po' Boy: Of course you're dressed!

Veggie: Spray the popcorn with soy sauce first?

REVEAL 77: **Dimension**

Point: Massage chairs collocation online dating

Height: Didn't work?

Width: By the padding edge of the ancestor

Depth: Ski and snow conditions

Time: Disable animation

5?: And dive in

6?: Learn more about surfing

7?: Without fighting through the clutter

8?: Of language, theme, violence, and sex

9?: Get a dream girl mobile

10?: Explore an alternative route into nursing

REVEAL 78: **Faucet**

Hot: In the yellow box, click to rate the photo

    See what others thought on the left. Repeat.

Cold: Cherry noted that corrosive is the single best word

    Holy Shit! I never expected you to say something like that!

REVEAL 79: Consonant

B: Discriminatory road regime changes the barrier

C: Just create a synthetically pleasing remake of a pop hit

D: To drive rhapsody service to any television

F: Today you came into work looking very tan

G: Don't throw anything away. Keep it all in context

H: A network on architectural stained glass

J: Is pot coming between you and a friend?

K: In conjunction with absolute zero

L: Concrete proposals will be made

M: And useful telephone numbers

N: By subject, grade level, and format tools

P: To announce our content improved!

Q: Knickknacks! Get your freak on!

R: Can be considered as a different implementation of

S: Pro pro plus and pro premium searches

T: Love to talk? Take lots of pictures?

V: Find out more about watch fire's enterprise

W: And wheel around their hometowns from now

X: Join the o pen mirror

Y: And play silent sometimes

Z: Target these risks and help

REVEAL 80: Radio

AM: A pool of gliding swirls and pads is tropical
FM: On a spicy trip of truly titanic proportions

REVEAL 81: **Square**

1: The complete guide to spelling…

4: Not all boys will be boys…

9: More than $100 and therefore it's theft…

16: Entire generations just won't grow…

25: Press search and whammo…

36: Jerk schedules, mating rituals, where we'll be drinking, etc…

49: Heroism with bruising emotional force…

64: Touching is good. No, really…

81: Covers were laid for…

100: A secret in a moonlit skyscraper…

REVEAL 82: ZOO

Flamingo: Muscle relief for arms and legs

Elephant: Except that it's not

Lemur: In fact, when I first went into this bit of forest

Tiger: A sliding puzzle game!

Panda: Don't wait any longer and choose

Bat: From seed to smoke

Orangutan: In the form of palm oil plantations

Baboon: Patches of bright red, blue, or purple

Bongo: Also one of the pillars

Giraffe: To dissect into intricate tapestry by patches

Zebra: And eliminate trips to a central location

Rhino: Curves, surfaces, and solids in windows

Ostrich: To ensure the long-term viability

Lion: What's a motto with you?

REVEAL 83: **Presidents**

Access is vice; search one act
Angle first concert two
Store quality guest
Proteome
Privacy focus finds daily specialists and juice
Stress brought
Event situations update white
Atomic bison of industry
Lecture the past and
World straps our
Key tour hopeful
And updated
Little

REVEAL 84: Condiments

Mustard: Adds bounce to the female fitness craze

Ketchup: Many have already been answered

Relish: Has been split into multiple pages

Hot Sauce: Adorned with a golden bullet on a key chain

Soy Sauce: Highlights the simple elegance of blending

Salt: Mined by the room and pillar method

Pepper: Arrangements of a Christmas standard

Horseradish: Bellows to Blondie during one, stormy

REVEAL 85: **Body**

Head: From birth to age 5, pregnant women and their families
Shoulder: With other practices across the country
Knee: As you walk, run, and jump
Toe: Slowly creeping forth and north
Eye: Writes to Dear Abby
Ear: Under normal circumstances this honeycombed area
Mouth: Put on for you plump, moisturized, and enhanced
Nose: I guess it's worth it. Jump

REVEAL 86: **Bolt**

Locked: How to plan a sensational sleepover
Unlocked: Full dual head video in the new
Lightning: Glass channels that are normally hollow

REVEAL 87: **Herb**

Tarragon: Have you seen Helen's necklace?
Parsley: We destroy sacred spaces when we build
Sage: The power of many in a common pylon
Rosemary: Read her your "read to your bunny" message
Thyme: And related forms in Hebrew and Persian
Cilantro: Aphrodisiac soil should be kept moist
Mint: Follow the trail, catch magpies, string beads
Chervil: By deep-freezing or by making
Chive: The glow of the bar, the dramatic stage
Bay: A rustic bear bench for your lodge

REVEAL 88: **Knot**

Square: Odd lots can now be rounded up

Overhand: Use a proper whipping in all other cases

Bowline: It has the advantage of not jamming

Sheet-Bend: That is, repeating steps 3-4

Reef: Palm tree management, salty cooling

Clove Hitch: It won't unroll and is easier to finish

Two Half Hitches: Bring the bitter end over the standing part

Tautline Hitch: When pressure is applied, it won't get smaller

Splice: No bullshit. Eight bucks a night

Tie: A box of angels forms in the valley

Windsor: Taking vehicle safety on the road

Noose: If I suck enough lemons, my face will implode

REVEAL 89: **Shakespeare**

Othello: Like what you see?

Hamlet: With its myriad meanings

Macbeth: And if that's not enough

Lear: Interiors advance relentlessly

Tempest: Through a fiberglass panel

As You Like It: From the stalling of an ox

Winters Tale: And discussing the weather

Much Ado: To Buffy the vampire slayer

Troilus: Made available in six parts

Cymbeline: Three sisters introduced to the color red

Coriolanus: Offer to take notes for you?

Taming: We don't want a bullet in front

Timon: Of the sect of skeptics

Henry V: Having never seen the child

REVEAL 90: **Mark**

Period: Feeling tired, cranky, and worn out?
Comma: The quickest way to get fresh with your car
Colon: We invite you to explore!
Semicolon: Enthusiasts should try Agnes
Question: If the area of the shaded region is 20n
Exclamation: That creeps me out a bit
Dash: It's not enough to tell hypertensive patients
Hyphen: Tokyo 2040 and her swank red jacket
Quotation: Let the fists do the talkin'
Parenthesis: Delicate boy, eccentric flower
Ampersand: What if it freezes that way?

REVEAL 91: **Bowling**

Frame: The user selects a rattlesnake from the table of contents

Strike: How many times do you have to be screwed?

Spare: Use an electric or old-fashioned push lawnmower

Mark: Preferably one that doesn't involve angle brackets

Split: From our perfect fit bottoms with detailing

REVEAL 92: Current

AC: Created in the shape of an ostrich

DC: A celebrity murder! A sea of Hollywood sharks!

REVEAL 93: **Name**

Smith: The women instinctively flock like salmon

Johnson: Various options exist to perpetuate the lynx

Williams: According to the provisional calendar for 2012

Jones: Experts say we're about to run out of oil

Brown: But I like ensembles, and I like public work

Davis: Veterinarians help determine why porpoises died

Miller: And close the case to win a bobcat

Wilson: Its key role in solar activity

Moore: Like a rollercoaster ride from hell

Taylor: Noise reduction essential

Anderson: For twenty years on glass

Thomas: Put chalk on the tracks

Jackson: Angle and sixth right diaphragm

White: As a pedestrian park Tuesday

Harris: To digital on your timetable

REVEAL 94: Citrus

Orange: Pick an inbox, any inbox
Lemon: I have always liked this game
Lime: Cleaner interface with skin, but no Trojan horse
Grapefruit: Believed to be a spontaneous sport
Tangerine: You virtually ripped the 200 limited
Kumquat: In all the ways your imagination will allow

REVEAL 95: Humidity

Dry: Its legends of pirates and sunken gold
Wet: Traded in his empire of beaver pelts

REVEAL 96: Scale (2)

Richter: Let's imagine a chunk of rock

Musical: And the amazing technicolor dreamcoat

12-Tone: Arranged under various headings

1 to 10: Ok, big boy, do you have what it takes?

Dragon: World soccer, pocket armor, royal Hong Kong police

Libra: Is your karma hurting you?

Justice: Burn a signal fire to watch

Model: A fully automated protein structure

Weight: To help you manage hundreds of delicious

Map: Airports to local businesses

Bathroom: Even intrepid travelers prefer

Time: The most accurate, current, local

Large: Peachy keen and up to snuff

Built to: At the Egyptian theater in Boise

REVEAL 97: **Freud**

Id: Our friends across the pond

Ego: Discount the joke of the day

Superego: Associated with the dread of castration

REVEAL 98: **Organ**

Intestine: It folds many times to fit

Pancreas: Cells that are indeterminate

Stomach: What are the key statistics?

Appendix: With limited support for Boolean attributes

Colon: Each day for seven days

Liver: A synthesis & breakdown of complex triangles

Spleen: To the resident B-cells for a match

Gall Bladder: A special system has evolved for their absorption

Duodenum: So long as we are here

REVEAL 99: **Grain**

Wheat: Teenage girls, sedentary men
Rice: The shape of things at eight
Corn: An experimental field
Oats: Earn one point for every $25 you spend
Barley: To ensure a daily morning bowl
Rye: Now that the days of defense are over
Sorghum: Cash in on the yield contest!
Millet: Equipment mountain, clothing mountain
Spelt: An interval of caramel foretold

REVEAL 100: **Elements (2)**

Fire: Prepare for unexpected events

Air: Activity breaks on sale now

Water: With a diagram available in 36 languages

Earth: Or even with just your own eyes

REVEAL 101: **Fasteners**

Glue: With a zealous commitment to

Screw: In a gear train a worm gear

Hinge: H-spot on cloud nine

Nail: Enter tooth &

Velcro: From a number of resins &

Staple: Not so glitzy as some

Brace: Through grade twelve, achieve

Biscuit: Four diamonds on my grave

Paperclip: Have you checked with our family of?

REVEAL 102: **Keyboard**

1234567890: Traffic exchange, stormpay randomizer
QWERTYUIOP: Ever wonder what goes on in that little booth?
ASDFGHJKL: Stewardess shows flaws in the alternation
ZXCVBNM: Two million points; ten million g-flops

REVEAL 103: Furniture

Couch: Are you ready to clown around?

Chair: Take this groovy tour to ponder the answer

Cabinet: And, by law, the heads of fifteen

Shelf: Quite attractive, one convert tells why

Desk: Some 200 oystermen work the reefs

Table: Sail the space between the cell walls

Dresser: From gasoline to decorative mirrors

REVEAL 104: OZ

Dorothy: Contact us, mystery shopper!

Scarecrow: A place of petty rivalries, bad flirting, & bruised egos

Tinman: Vaguely house-like beats and breathy flashes

Lion: Puppy club, what's new & in season?

Wizard: Bundle up and play in the snow

Witch: The creek is clogged with oily bundles of sticks

Toto: I hear the same old fourteen reasons

REVEAL 105: Fashion

Products feature humans missing nine dollars
Win growing contests together
Your rep line united city
To shop now movie message
Students may help game pro
Line 919 to album biographies
More about possible television
Film-ball, acrobat-filled wallpaper
Select earth's biggest united state
And anonymous plans the date
Personalize searches eleven carts welcome
Day's kingdom cork applies Paris
Of sound, deepest, free-moving other

REVEAL 106: **Record**

33: They were airports for shadows and for dust

45: Old hat shops, broken bits of chrome, faded whitewash

78: Backed by a chorus of pressing men

REVEAL 107: Shade (2)

Chartreuse: The secret manuscript became liqueur

Emerald: Within two easy-to-use toolkits

Kelly: Driving away as soon as tomorrow

Olive: To enter your customized garden

Pea: The kitchen council, the dock, the market

Turquoise: 6000-foot walls, eagle rays

Teal: Connect falling conduit pieces to explosive loops

Lime: The end of the beginning

REVEAL 108: Symbol

Wheel: Winter…it's around the corner
Conch: So let yourself go and fall under the spell
Flag: Images reflect the change in connection speeds
Umbrella: Who cares if she gives them a blowjob?
Fish: Belly up and grab a cozy spot
Lotus: Want to see Elise in blue?
Vase: She is not quite a sexless tube, although her arms
Knot: Everything you need for weddings

Ms: However, there are many ways you can improve your memory

Mr: Bad things and bad houses in particular seem to hunger for small children

Dr: Like Fibonacci, fractal, or proof. We called them the "Swat Team"

REVEAL 110: Stroke

Back: Tables groan under coconuts, jackets, radishes, & potatoes
Breast: The beauty of jade is fun, feminine, pink!
Butterfly: Is frantic wriggling normal?
Crawl: Bite the hand that bleeds
Side: Netting too provides an easy event

REVEAL 111: **Home**

Aviary: Over 600 exotic & endangered admission for one
Sanctuary: Nor simply what relish, what responsibilities
Zoo: To create a customized village, our gift shop
Sanitarium: Prefer a better life to better snack foods

REVEAL 112: Sea

South China: Deadly cobras, threat to survivors
Caribbean: (This map is not to scale)
Mediterranean: 51 panoramic, interactive walkthroughs
Bering: And 11, street of the grazing ground
Okhotsk: Sound rockets reach altitudes of 1,000k
Andaman: A helicopter tracks colored air
Black: Did you know E. G. Becket invented the mailbox?
Red: The oracle's goal is to provide a high
North: As lab performs research angels
Baltic: At the heart of the regeneration of gate

REVEAL 113: Fiction

Is there a map of Maycomb and moved into a cold-water apartment with makeshift furniture? Where other women dared not to tread, fourteen artists have been invited to explore. Clinging to each other in their loneliness and alienation. Rooted in the earth and the people. Believing in the green light, the orgiastic future that year by year recedes before us portrays them as uncritical revelers. A brief read through other areas might clear up any confusion, as well as a three-dimensional rendering of the island. The obscene sales prospectus illustrates (like any soap service-derived implementation) the match of the target endpoint. Relax. We're here to help navigate a nice letter from a lawyer for her wall. If only people would look at her, the 2008 Beijing Olympics would revolve around a predominant oak tree overhanging a creek. And Buddy Hackett ain't nowhere in sight! Eventually his father was sent to debtor's prison, and characters were brought together as a sequel.

REVEAL 114: Map

Latitude: Hey! Wait a minute!
    It was in the zodiac constellation of Aries, the ram
Longitude: Trying to picture gridirons & grasshoppers
    & how everything came together
    Movements to do away with friction

REVEAL 115: **Pattern**

Stripe: Check out some other models in the picture

Solid: To ensure they are not communicating with strangers

Spot: What does this phone number spell?

Plaid: Her head nestled in lemons at heaven's door

Paisley: A pickle, a pear, a mango or a twisted raindrop

Herringbone: Or, if not, just get measured up correctly

Check: 66% suffer internal attacks

Geometric: For solid edge joins solid edge

Abstract: Eeny, meeny, miny, mo

REVEAL 116: Choice

Rock: To be there in different flavors and degrees
Paper: A compact web, which can then be macerated
Scissors: But don't eat the little mint

REVEAL 117: **Holiday**

Champagne: Explorer selection, immediate boarding

Heart: Attack & act quickly when you notice the warning

Egg: Make yours a double; get 20 a virgin

Fireworks: But don't be surprised if the cops show up

Pumpkin: Winter snow, ice damage, deer, & rabbits

Turkey: Follow the results of the referenda held in Cyprus

Tree: Females secrete a thin shell in which they reside

Brave: Let's kiss! No, that's not a proposal!

Philly: Come for the brews, stay for the food!

Marlin: Are peep or tang sites available for my lever?

Met: Although anger increasingly came to dislike

Expo: Never going out of style, small appliances

Cardinal: Improve efficiency all along the chain of care

Astro: What lies behind this changeability?

Cub: Who the hell do you think you are, spoonbender?

Red: First they ignore you. Then they laugh at you

Pirate: When you talk about yourself in the third person

Brewer: Time no longer matters

Dodger: And their respective mascots split

Giant: Don't be afraid. It's actually pretty easy

Padre: Break community caroling at the lighthouse

Rocky: To fight the heavyweight champ

Diamondback: Keep the spring in your step and check out

REVEAL 119: Circus

Juggler: Warming up numbers, mill's mess
Clown: Adding a swatch of color to a sea of black
Acrobat: Choose your language, speed, & paper
Ring: For daughter, fearing comma's full
Animal: Eavesdrop with tools a double agent would love

REVEAL 120: Phone

1: Winter testing continued at the circuit

2ABC: It tends to cream the bottom while the top stays chunky

3DEF: Preliminary maps of surficial sediment flower

4GHI: What is going on with cockpit?

5JKL: Dynamic voting booth for on-spot results

6MNO: Antique, veneered, or wooden surfaces

7PRS: Auto-generated by our shopping cart

8TUV: And you cannot try this landscape?

9WXY: It never really leaks out onto the grass like a garden hose

*: Few offer platinum around the clock

0: The crunchy manufacturer of all-natural toothpaste

#: Without cheesy music (unless it's yours)

REVEAL 121: **Metal**

Lead: Such as spinach and dairy products

Iron: Seven generations from Adam

Mercury: & place it squarely at the top of the food chain

Aluminum: Novel approaches provide myriad benefits

Magnesium: To see the results of getting off

Nickel: From two mandolin instrumentals

Zinc: Comprised of primary and secondary producers

Copper: Stemming from asterisk cleansers

Silver: Crystals suspended on unexposed film

Gold: Used to power super-thin screens

Platinum: Your little strip of choice

REVEAL 122: **Power**

On: A fashion collective works in a silver-painted loft

Off: Push, pull, crawl: Do whatever it takes to get there

REVEAL 123: **Speech**

Noun: We feel burglarized of 365 days to the meter

Pronoun: Who do you think is responsible?

Verb: If you're still making snow angels, you'd better step up

Adjective: The truck-shaped balloon floats over the treetops

Adverb: The images on the negative appear dark

Preposition: Is there a post office on the table?

Conjunction: The interval determining the coincidence gate is adjustable

Interjection: As I entered the room—Oh my God, what I saw!

REVEAL 124: Accessory

Hat: They inhaled fumes from mercury
Scarf: To show the right side and wrong side
Tie clip: Milling machine or shiny moustache
Glove: Who can't go back to Jersey
Bracelet: Have you cuffed anyone in the last 24 hours?
Belt: Aware of a vast population of small bodies?
Cufflink: Imagine timeless manhole covers
Necklace: Imagine vast saloons with antique silks
Earring: Beauty inspires obsession
Purse: To the dark corners, still accepting

REVEAL 125: Infection

C((nt((r f((((r B(((m Phys(((cs (CBP) (r((d((s(((gn(((ng (l(s((rdr(((v((n(cc((l((r(t((((r th(t c(n d((l(((v((r s(((((ff(((c(((((nt (m((((((((((nts ((((fr(d(((((((((((s((((t((((p((s f((((r m((d(((c(l (((((s((. (((f s(((((cc((ssf(((((l, th((r((s(((rch w(((((((((ld r((s(((((lt (((n (c((((mp(ct m(ch(((n((th(t c((((((((((ld b(((((((s((d b((((th f((((r r(d(((((((th((r(py (nd f((((r pr((((d(((((c(((ng r(d((((((((((s((((t((((p((s (t l((((w((r c((((st, ((n(bl(((ng w(((d((r (((((s((.

REVEAL 126: **Egg**

Hardboiled: You dumb mug, get your mitts off the marbles!
Softboiled: Bruce, forget store-bought candy!
Scrambled: Click on the head or tail to change
Poached: Or check out these features:
Over Easy: Wolfpack, hopple popple, inner circle a mile high,
Over Hard: The sweetest young lady in the known cosmos!
Sunny Side Up: Poems demonstrating the true beauty of
Omelet: Knock him down! Punch left! Punch right!

Yankee: Research showcase demystifies the next generation

Red Sock: With the usual random thoughts & self-indulgent claptrap

Oriole: Dull yellowish-orange coverts gray, breast and undertail

Devil Ray: Inks three others, jumps to official bell

Blue Jay: Hall-worthy zone declines down signs

Twin: On a hot sauce bottle? You bet!

White Sock: Reduces irritation caused by friction

Indian: A new road for a legendary ride

Tiger: Lists give the environment some festive cheer

Royal: Depending on its ability to commercialize

Angel: Tide works wonders & this year's nominations gotcha!

Athletic: The night commission calls for rates to factor

Ranger: Delivering contingency paybacks in competitive fishing!

Mariner: Filled to the crow's nest with prized artifacts

Classical: Many people devote their lives to studying obscure facets

Jazz: A couple of weeks ago Concord bought new skin

Rock: Roebuck "Pops" Staples was born in Winona, Mississippi

Pop: The more you know, the more you know

Folk: The reorganization is almost complete

Country: No butterflies or dandelions or something soft

Indie: Club gunman off his rocker, says ex-friend

Hip Hop: What is preemptive hype? Boom!!

REVEAL 129: Lumber

Fir: "Do as infinity" compares to "fairyland in reality"
Pine: Today there is virtually no elm code left
Poplar: Stringed instruments are made with one-piece backs
Cedar: On a small side-wheel steamer, the young reindeer
Ash: Has joined the elite cadre who perform in dreams
Birch: A plan by vampires to resurrect Dracula
Oak: Increases the availability of clean, abundant energy
Maple: Deploys rock-solid numerics and world-class symbolics
Walnut: Consistent with the circulation of the general plan
Cherry: Snap-action & rocker switches, magnetic splashwheels
Teak: Are provided as necessary (all packed in plastic)
Mahogany: And for all of them, full mime support

REVEAL 130: **Tooth**

Incisor: The speculation over whether it will float is over
Canine: Shake hands and exchange pleasantries
Bicuspid: The opening of two leaflets creates a fish mouth
Molar: And presto, you have an agent of bananas
Wisdom: He resigns from the herd and thinks for himself

REVEAL 131: Degree

AA: To avoid toll roads and congestion charging

BA: Take the controls of a competitive flight simulator

BS: Full screen skin can now be top and bottom

MBA: Not sure where to begin? Tell us a little about yourself

MFA: High style and hoop skirts through March 31st

MA: Where to pick your own peaches and certs

MS: A cheat sheet: How portals helped break through walls

MD: The most common side effect is heartbreak

JD: With a customer satisfaction index score of 630

PhD: Electron band structure in germanium, my ass

Belgium: It happens time after time

France: All clips in integrality

Germany: From the exciting hustle

Italy: About expositions, museums, and other

Luxembourg: It lost more than half

Netherlands: The award-winning airport

Denmark: I'm traveling from

Ireland: Indices of recent publications

United Kingdom: In general

Greece: Completely lacking in metal resources

Spain: Dates back to cave paintings

Portugal: Rattling streets framed by looms

Austria: Status remained unclear for a decade

Finland: Among its carnival of words

Sweden: Until evening to hand out presents

Cyprus: And acts of self-defense

Czech Republic: In what is the first major

Estonia: Limit fixed in coordination

Hungary: You click on a red triangle

Latvia: Or to the depth of exploitation

Lithuania: Many scattered small lakes

Malta: Get around by horse-drawn karrozin

Poland: A shock therapy program

Slovakia: The velvet divorce

Slovenia: What's cooking

REVEAL 133: Room

Bed: Or let us prepare one for you, printed in full color
Bath: Your jigsaw strategy could lead to arguments
Living: Two lines, up to 8 characters each
Dining: With sweet flesh and gentle crunch
Kitchen: Turn on the remote
Study: Know exactly what you are supposed to do

REVEAL 134: Spice

Anise: After mention of Dioscorides & Pliny

Cardamom: Start with surnames in the family tree

Cinnamon: And a worthy sequel to nonsense

Clove: There has been an amazing drop on blue

Coriander: And waste places by the sides of rivers

Cumin: This may lead to considerable confusion. For example,

Dill: Research in asynchronous circuit verification

Ginger: Demonstrates the vision to bridge the last mile

Marjoram: Often in conjunction with qualifying adjectives

Nutmeg: And dipped in lime to prevent their growth

Pepper: Blue horizon, good shit. I drove from 11 to 3

Saffron: Both for its filaments and for its tin

Sesame: For the chance to ride the rotten bumper cars

Turmeric: And feel the radical warmth in my mouth

REVEAL 135: **Stoplight**

Stop: Don't forget about canned fruits and food safety

Go: Learn how to tackle nursing strikes

Caution: Supernatural rioting can occur at any time

REVEAL 136: **Toolbox**

Hammer: My chemical romance is going to be filming
Saw: Chained to opposite sides of the room
Wrench: With a running tally of weights
Awl: Art fulfillments and oasis, the best account
Screwdriver: Twig's distribution tarred then zipped
File: By tuxedo from the bad law department
Pliers: Super copper, chain compression, 9.0 inches
Plane: Axis on more sticks & yokes, a scenery upgrade
Chisel: Of summer flame trees, standing
Sandpaper: Up from a number of sharp edges

REVEAL 137: **Altitude**

High: Tiger beat the blunt smoking featherweight

Low: Lion/lamb blowing in the 11 turning over

REVEAL 138: **Monster**

Minotaur: Together, they wheeled it into the pasture

Basilisk: Port Poseidon's pickles are low end

Dragon: With a removable upper shell

Ghost: To reinvent the world's mating rituals

Medusa: In which he'd chanced to catch a glimpse

Chimera: What the latest nightly builds become

Hydra: The only collaborative one you can actually use

Werewolf: Just outside of town where a candle always burns

Leviathan: And the nerves with so many strings

Centaur: Not five pages from my calendar

Harpy: But from the brow of her mother

Griffin: Cool shark with time-shift recording

Doppelganger: Invisible to human eyes

Golem: Do you not know where Prague is located?

REVEAL 139: Storage

Bit: You're running. Explain exactly what behavior you're seeing

Byte: Defending against oracle attacks is easy—but only if you see

MB: Engineer moments of pure elation. It sure sounds yummy

GB: For you, baby: The return of cabaret girls & black jack tables

Bin: Shoot the watermelon!

Box: Wine and dark chocolate for better random freaky!

Folder: If you have any brilliant (or even marginal) ideas

Closet: You've come to the right place for dirt

REVEAL 140: **Constellation**

Ursa Major: And the dipper's cup is the bear's flank
Ursa Minor: Caused by the gravitational attraction
Orion: Quick! Wizard Q&A will lead you to the right
Andromeda: To see the countdown if you live outside
Gemini: Out where your relationship is headed
Crux: A relatively small collection of trimmed packages
Draco: Was shown many times (upside down)
Eridanus: A piglet clings to the white of the page
Libra: You're able to shape events by going along with them
Cassiopeia: Sweep the region with an opera glass
Ara: Enhance blast protection during explosion
Perseus: What did an educated Roman know about the world?
Taurus: 24/7. Fill your hand. Find the perfect firearm
Cetus: The object-oriented paradigm turned to stone

REVEAL 141: **Utensil (2)**

Whisk: Check out the benefits of belonging

Spatula: But first make sure you read the warnings

Peeler: Beyond this page, you agree to abide by

Tong: A small case of the silverstone previously shown

Grater: Shading has been added to improve visibility

Sifter: We'll turn napkins into unified field theories

Measuring Spoon: Green, pink, blue, purple, & black

Colander: With a methodology appropriate to policy

Rolling Pin: Applying was never simple! Where's my next kiosk?

Can Opener: The first were very thick and had to be hammered

Ladle: Comb ink, sweat hard. Disgracing is verse

REVEAL 142: **Trigonometry**

Sin: Bulletproof jackets, work with us

Cos: The golden ratio melts into metallic tape

Tan: & the good thief. All feast days are marked

Arcsin: Have branch-cut discontinuities in the complex z-plane

Arccos: Zeros (one formula); history (zero formulas)

Arctan: Overused and underappreciated. Right?

REVEAL 143: Shade (3)

Rose: Due to the high elevations and dry climate
Salmon: There will be lots of young eyes lurking
Peach: But all of the girls want you to pick them
Crimson: Fast in loading time, but small in size
Scarlet: A breathy little exhalation like a snake's hiss
Vermillion: Is tapped into the pulse of the core
Tangerine: This is bound to change
Brick: Garden of Eden, Sodom & Gomorrah
Burgundy: Long-lasting alchemy of initiation
Rust: The flavor of red and moisture

REVEAL 144: Size

S: Strange how sparks venture into dares

M: No longer represent any specific words

L: The scene of frequent and bloody wars

XL: Can't stretch the artform without straining

XXL: Tugs on the ear of the return

REVEAL 145: **Orinthology**

Eagle: Imported spices maximize your voltage output

Hawk: With its mountaintop vistas and thrilling mitigation

Crow: The first cut is the deepest

Tanager: Available to a broad spectrum

Grackle: In cottonwood forests and sycamore groves

Robin: Unbridled in everything they do

Sparrow: Are you at risk?

Swallow: A lot of cream plus points and forks

Owl: Such as commas and appositives

Vulture: Bake off the few bits of fuzz

Lark: A beautifully crafted 6-hole ocarina

Loon: At gravity's mountainous playground

Starling: (Not evident in the fall)

Waxwing: Just pray you don't break tonight

REVEAL 146: Instrument

Sax: Reports parse events and don't usually build an internal tree
Zither: Which stretches over a chamber but doesn't extend beyond
Violin: Hopefully more comprehensive in times to come
Guitar: The velocity of a dice roll is addictive
Drum: Check out the pearl's edge
Piano: A boycott of another's

Scalpel: Imagine if doctors found a mysterious object in your body
Clamp: It's dense, with a postcard storyline
Microscope: From the milky way down through to a single proton
Calculator: Time functions & has a stopwatch
Pencil: Scribes write on papyrus
Compass: & prepare to take off

REVEAL 147: **Fortune**

The radio timeline's in the materials
General info, conservation program advocacy
Photos go jump trust relations
Just to leading box and space administration
Who premieres a social communication
Suffers from nine information about
Work and its interests to unite
Run seven corporate and more
Structure echo's friendly home for experience

REVEAL 148: Court

District: To plant cherry trees along the waterfront

Superior: To see galaxies, planets, and nebulae

State: To receive a transparent tool

Appeals: To request a ticket for better hearing

Federal: To get the creditors off his back

Supreme: To ordain and establish

Tennis: To be able to challenge the judgments of the linemen

REVEAL 149: **Disaster**

Fire: Perhaps because candles are frequently a part of holiday rituals

Tornado: Give the subject a different twist. You'll be glad you blew

Earthquake: In a crustal structure & borehole physics

Flood: Some stretches as much as 60% by weight

Hurricane: Our tropical graphics evacuate our aircraft out of harm's way

Landslide: Stockpiling waste piles may stress weak slopes

Blizzard: Replace those visions of sugarplums dancing in your head

REVEAL 150: Range

Clean: With its folds of jewels and herbs
Dirty: Sweets that are not eaten by elapsing

Happy: Cute, cuddly, and horribly wrong
Sad: The lack of sunlight in winter for many

Big: The right place to find and be found
Little: To write each word, and one is missing

REVEAL 151: **Measure**

League: How many votes is a picture worth?

Knot: How do I hide the tattoo on my shoulder?

Horsepower: Most lawn mowers have a big sticker on them

Newton: In particular of clocks and windmills

Shot: A chance for additional exposure

Caliber: Staff around eight practice areas

Decibel: White light is a mix of all visible frequencies

Karat: & the rhinoceros adds and keeps gadgets

Ream: Calculated to the nearest one hundredth of a pound

Em: Try and execute the perfect volley

REVEAL 152: Light

Wave: Woman's voice: Are you still up?

    9-1-1 has been changed to an unpublished number

Particle: A very energetic version of the elevator

    See you across the pond again in March!

REVEAL 153: Island

Canary: In the streetscape, it is virtually impossible

Block: What can I do? Am I in trouble?

Long: Incubating in some form, the thickness of the line

Virgin: Hates all the other available heroes

Aleutian: If you can't find it on my big map

Easter: Visit our carrot patch and find out who is eating

Christmas: Pizza, chocolate, and the cigar of the month

Hawaii: Ever wonder about the real history of surfing?

Falkland: An outdoor scale model has been unveiled

Samoa: About one half of the way

REVEAL 154: Desert

Gobi: The last time I counted, there were 14 takhi
Death Valley: Morning light crept across the eroded badlands
Mojave: Carpeted with vivid, a network of dirt
Sahara: Launches a steel fare scheme. Cosmos member?
Painted: Remember the beatings when the streetlights went out?
Sonoran: This phenomenon is not limited to here

REVEAL 155: **Storm**

Arlene: 17 agents with over 125 years combined

Bret: So far 18,959 people have taken this particular

Cindy: Placing among the top 15, appearing on over 600

Dennis: As violent or repressive responses, a 100% windfall

Emily: Rippin' 56, I don't do weekdays, 22 strange until

Franklin: More than 22,000 in 15 days, 11th providing instant

Gert: Originally intended to run from 1998 to 2000

Harvey: Finland, S; Sweden, 15; USA, certificate 14694

Irene: IE 5.5 or higher; 545,269 visits since last

Jose: 30 percent Beethoven center; 20-year reading discussion

Katrina: 3, Vicky felt moved to buy the local biweekly newspaper

Katrina: 3.2 million overnight stays at 1,150 shelters across 27 states

Lee: Overall $54,000,000 in exchange for a $5 donation

Maria: 1 Points: 4,768; Yearly: 3 Points: 3,199

Nate: 430,000 are invited to have their say on the revision

Ophelia: Generally agreed to be somewhere from 16-19

Philippe: Found search 3 [100%] hits 11 [100%]

Rita: In the new world some 200 years before California

Stan: To buy a dozen fresh eggs, but when they get there

Tammy: Headed east on Interstate 66, a major highway

Vince: 29 per ticket and all proceeds go to aim

Wilma: Cloud 9, 9 parts desire, I am my own wife

REVEAL 156: Chromosome

XX: All that remains is for hire or script
XY: Briefs or boxers? Are you depressed?

Poker (2)

High: Such as coins, or by cutting out paper shapes

Pair: Is the Flash headed for retirement?

2 Pair: With copper vision and a breathable frequency

3 of a Kind: I can see it gleaming in the mist

Straight: Was Boston once literally flooded with molasses?

Flush: Do you know your Dada from your MoMA?

Full House: The milkman and the paperboy

4 of a Kind: Might be delivered in place of one another

Straight Flush: Ranking is determined by the value of the high

Royal Flush: Incline, tilt sensitivity, flipper power, and more

REVEAL 158: **Flower**

Tulip: On the other hand, for the added branch
Rose: The dappled confusion of the neglected corner
Bluet: Uses many vintage fabrics
Crocus: & wheelbarrow giftwrapping
Snapdragon: The arrows set the hands
Hollyhock: An eclectic mix of the 18th & 19th centuries
Narcissus: All woven with impossible embraces
Ladyslipper: & dedicating a brick to a couple
Peony: Or the stigma of a seashell. Athena
Daisy: Introduces a new idea to the windmill

REVEAL 159: **Fruit**

Cherry: Get the scoop on smoke & bubblegum culture

Melon: Too much, too much, too much lemonade

Banana: Grown from a purveyor of safari-inspired

Pineapple: Delicate meshes embellished with embroidery & lace

Lychee: Like martinis. They will absolutely love martinis

Pomegranate: & islands for the adventures of famous architects

Peach: They'll stop at nothing to win your heart

Pear: In the form of so-called "packages"

Plum: Fatigue in the background morning glories

Fig: A tough neck & neck for the balls & ribbons

Mango: With an average age of 30 and 82% female

Apple: To say it struck a chord would be to put it mildly

Kiwi: An icon & an oddity, this flightless, nocturnal

Persimmon: Has a stainless steel hob and extractor hood

REVEAL 160: **Vegetable**

Asparagus: Outdoor temperatures determine how much time
Cucumber: Insects will serve as the pollen carriers
Carrot: Pale fleshed & acrid, a far cry from wild ancestors
Celery: And derived from the Ancient Greek
Pea: Cool nights & nutrition-rich volcanic soils
Artichoke: Marilyn Monroe was crowned queen
Mushroom: Cameras & everything! Who loves chocolate?
Radish: When you discontinue corrections, memory leaks
Squash: On the planet. Throw open doors & stage a day
Lettuce: Stunted & bitter, stalk rapidly elongating forms
Spinach: The magical effects that Popeye enjoyed
Beet: For the running of the delta

REVEAL 161: **Coda**

Smell: Neon hates you South Carolina!
Skirt: Baking chocolate chip cookies for the very last guy
Pound: I won't even start on the virgin sacrifices!
Coco: Throw out a life jacket, as it were

Strange: There are 18 different animal shapes
Lake: Armed with a half-gallon of mouthwash
pt: Victim of intrigues guarantees eradication of the enslaved
23: Walk on the beach & kick your ass

Pirate: What's this "bathing" thing everyone's always telling me about?
Dorothy: In sizes 8 to 22, you'll have to be fast
Cilantro: An interesting to bolt (bolting is
0: The value of being the first down a dark alley

Turmeric: Tapering at each end, smooth, of a uniform green
Narcissus: Like the skin, frustrated by a film of water
Noun: This picture, this one of your secret garden
DC: Whatever happened to the first Mrs. Gordon?

Ampersand: Does a clown painting have as much value as a shower?
Clamp: Sweet underlay, sweet sewing update
Peach: Mosaic as one method to adhere
Leviathan: For seeing life is but a motion of limbs

NOTE FROM THE AUTHOR:

Reveal: All Shapes & Sizes is my fifth book of poetry, even though the bulk of the composition occurred in 2004. I began each poem by creating a cluster of keywords; I then completed each line with an "I'm Feeling Lucky" google search on that line's keyword. Each line, in other words, had a different vocabulary pallet (and often different rules for construction), although I quickly found that the pallets for each poem overlapped. My inspiration for the sequence's concept and process were John Cage and Ted Berrigan.

OTHER BOOKS BY BRUCE COVEY:

The Greek Gods as Telephone Wires (Front Room Publishers, out of print)
Elapsing Speedway Organism (No Tell Books, 2006)
Ten Pins, Ten Frames (Front Room, 2007)
Glass Is Really a Liquid (No Tell Books, 2010)